COLOURS

GREEN

Gabrielle Woolfitt

First published in Great Britain in 2016 by Wayland

Copyright © Wayland 2016

ISBN: 978 1 5263 0195 6

10 9 8 7 6 5 4 3 2 1

MIX
Paper from
responsible sources
FSC® C104740

Wayland
An imprint of
Hachette Children's Group
Part of Hodder & Stoughton
Carmelite House
50 Victoria Embankment
London EC4Y 0DZ

An Hachette UK Company
www.hachette.co.uk
www.hachettechildrens.co.uk
A catalogue for this title is available from the British Library

Printed and bound in China

Produced for Wayland by
White-Thomson Publishing Ltd
www.wtpub.co.uk

Editor: Izzi Howell
Designer: Rocket Design (East Anglia) Ltd
Picture researcher: Izzi Howell
Wayland editor: Vicky Brooker

The author Gabrielle Woolfitt is a qualified teacher,
specialising in science.

Every effort has been made to clear image copyright.
Should there be any inadvertent omission,
please apply to the publisher for rectification.

Picture acknowledgements:
The author and publisher would like to thank the following agencies
and people for allowing these pictures to be reproduced:

iStock: Rich Legg 7r, grafxart8888 10, Oliver Hoffmann 19t, vitranc
22, Juanmonino 28, Amanda Rohde 29b, &#169 Wojciech Gajda
30; Shutterstock: okawa somchai cover, ZaZa Studio title page,
Shebeko 4t, Nik Merkulov 4bl, Aleksey Stemmer 4bc, Nika Lerman
4br, Africa Studio 5, Ralf Gosch 6, SAHACHATZ 7l, majeczka 8–9,
mady70 11, TTphoto 12t, amenic181 12b, siete_vidas 13tl, Pavel
Vakhrushev 13tr, jmarkow 13b, Simon_g 14l, Dirk Ercken 14c, Hintau
Aliaksei 14r, vicspacewalker 15, welburnstuart16, Paul B. Moore 17,
Zeljko Radojko 18t, Alexander Mazurkevich 18b, Markuso 19bl, Maks
Narodenko 19br, ifong 20, Happy Together 21, Ekaterina Kondratova
23, Jaroslav Machacek 24, Marina Onokhiria 25t, JPC-PROD 25l, B and
E Dudzinscy 25r, Rich Carey 26tl, Paolo Bona 26tr, ratmaner26br,
wavebreakmedia 27, Laslo Ludrovan 29l, alphabe 29r, tobkatrina 31.

All design elements
from Shutterstock.

CONTENTS

WHAT IS GREEN?

Green is a natural colour. **PLANTS AND TREES** are green.

Lots of **VEGETABLES** are green.

This **SNAKE** has smooth green scales.

EMERALDS are green precious stones.

4

You can make green by **MIXING YELLOW** and **BLUE PAINT**. Try adding blue to yellow paint.

Only add a little each time. **WATCH THE COLOUR CHANGE** from lime green to leaf green and then to bottle green.

GREEN FOR GO!

Green is a **SAFETY COLOUR**. Green means go!

When the traffic light **CHANGES FROM YELLOW TO GREEN**, cars start to drive again.

The green man signal at the pedestrian crossing means it is **SAFE TO CROSS** the road – but **ALWAYS KEEP LOOKING!**

GREEN IN NATURE

Walk through a park on a sunny day.

Plants make their own food in their leaves. They need **SUNLIGHT, AIR** and **WATER.**

sycamore

Collect some
different
leaves.

maple

Find out
which leaf
comes from
which kind of
plant.

ash

Make a poster
to show what
you have
found out.

oak

GREEN COUNTRIES

It rains a lot in Ireland. The rain helps the grass to grow.

Ireland is sometimes called the **EMERALD ISLE** because it is so green.

This country is called **GREENLAND**.
It is a very cold, snowy island
It's not very green, is it?

Find out about other places with green in the name, such as **GREENWICH**.

GREEN GROWTH

In winter it is cold. The ground is hard.

There are only a few hours of sunlight each day. **PLANTS STOP GROWING.**

At the end of winter, tiny green shoots begin to poke through the earth. They grow into plants.

Soon new **GREEN SHOOTS** grow on bushes. **FLOWERS GROW** from the buds.

These flowers are snowdrops.

Spring is here!

GREEN ANIMALS

There are many green animals. Some jump, some fly and some crawl along the ground.

tree frog

dragonfly

Parrots have wings. They fly.

Squawk!

Think of some other green animals.

HOW DO THEY MOVE?

The **LIZARD** is green like the plant. It is hard to see.

A BIGGER ANIMAL might want to eat the lizard. But is it easy to find?

15

GREEN STORIES

Do you know the story of Jack and the beanstalk?

Fe Fi Fo Fum...

The beanstalk grows from a **MAGIC BEAN**.

When Jack climbs up the beanstalk, he meets a fierce giant. **FIND OUT WHAT HAPPENS NEXT.**

Have you heard the story of Robin Hood?

He lived in Sherwood Forest with his friends. They took money from rich people and gave it to poor people.

The rich people tried to stop them. But the forest was green and Robin Hood and his friends wore green clothes.

Why do you think it was hard to catch them?

UNRIPE GREEN

Most fruits and cereals are green while they are growing. They are unripe.

wheat

Oranges are green when they start to grow. As they ripen in the sun, they change colour. Then they are ready for picking.

You could not eat these **STRAWBERRIES**. They need more sunlight to help them ripen. What colour will the strawberries be when they are ripe?

Bananas are picked when they are still green.

They are sent on ships to the countries that buy them. When they arrive they have turned yellow. They are ready to eat.

GREEN FOOD

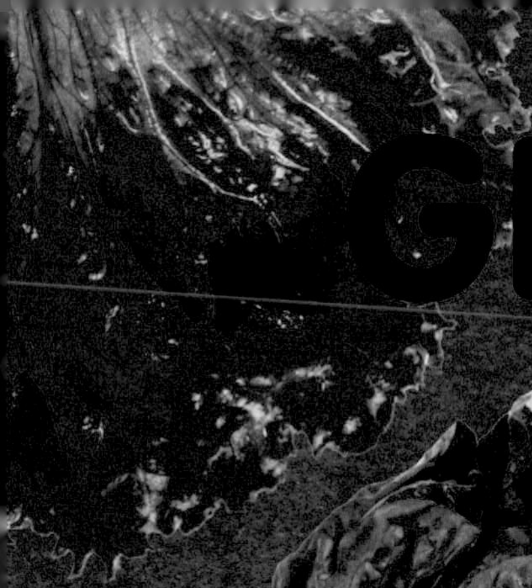

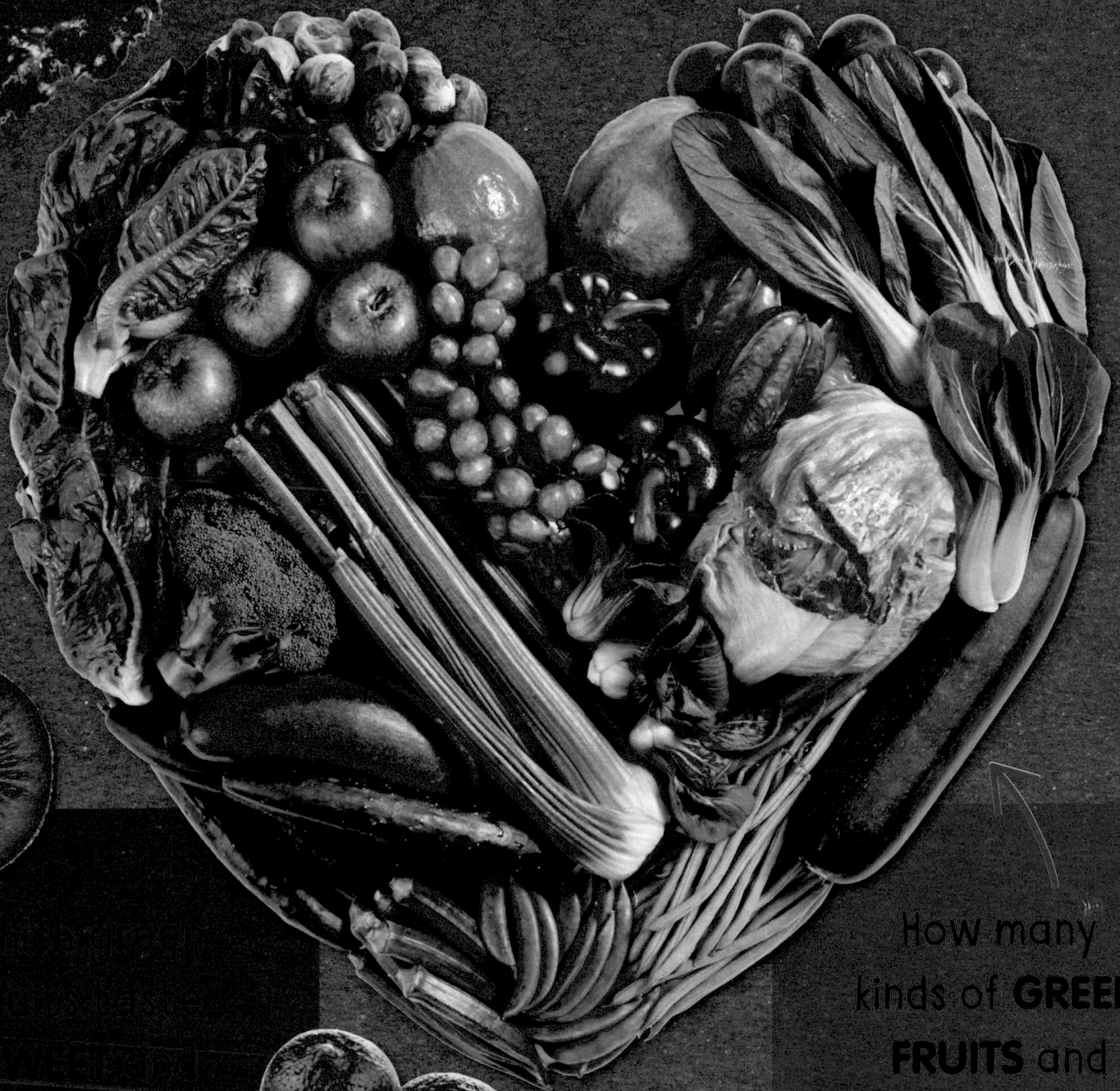

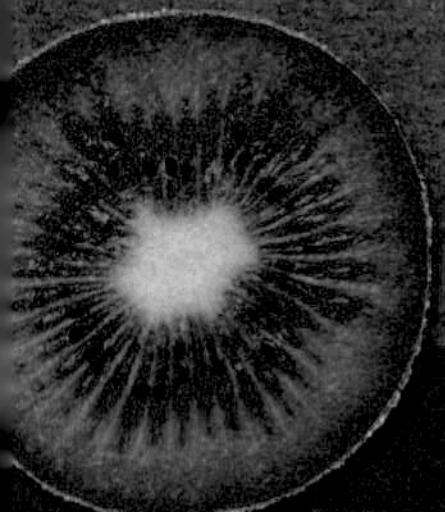

How many kinds of **GREEN FRUITS** and **VEGETABLES** can you name?

Which green fruits taste **SWEET** and which taste **SOUR?**

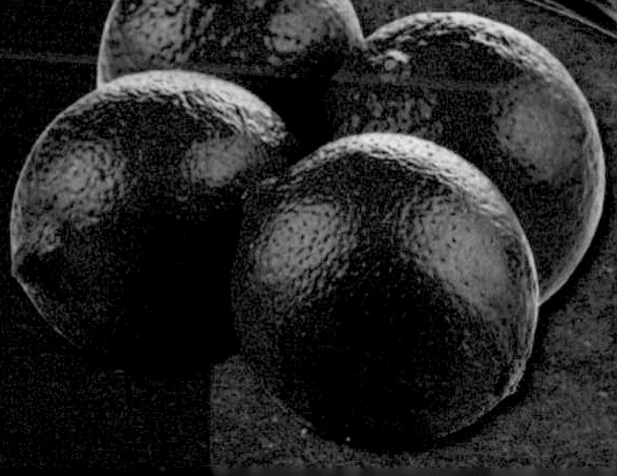

Which kinds of green food can you **EAT RAW?**

Which green foods could you **PUT IN A SALAD?**

Which green foods **ARE JUICY?**

Make a **CHART** to show which green foods your friends like best.

Crunch!

21

COOL GREEN

You can play in the cool green **SHADE** of a leafy tree.

Here is a recipe for a cool green summer drink.

1. Mix lime cordial with lemonade in a jug.

2. Put some ice cubes in each glass.

3. Pour the drink into the glasses. Decorate with a sprig of mint.

4. Add some slices of fresh lime to each glass.

GREEN HERBS

Herbs are special plants that are used for their **TASTE** and **AROMA**.

Many different **HERBS** grow in this garden.

MINT TEA is a very popular drink in Arab countries.

Mint can be made into sauce and served with **ROAST LAMB**.

Herbs have strong **FLAVOURS**. They can make food and drink taste **DELICIOUS**.

BASIL tastes good on **PIZZA**.

ROSEMARY OIL is used in some shampoos.

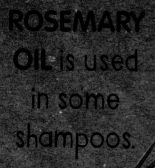

GREEN WORLD

Pollution makes the environment dirty. Your home and the places nearby are your **ENVIRONMENT**. Every person, animal and plant needs a clean environment.

CAR FUMES pollute the air. Pollution can kill living things.

LITTER is pollution.

People who look after their environment are often called **'GREEN'**.

SOME WAYS TO BE GREEN:

1. Don't drop litter.

2. Recycle empty bottles and tins.

3. Use recycled paper and reuse plastic bags.

What type of dinosaur is this?

GREEN MONSTERS

Millions of years ago dinosaurs lived on Earth. They were very large. Some dinosaurs were probably green. Dinosaurs have been extinct for a long time.

Lots of people tell stories about **DRAGONS**. Some dragons in stories are fierce and breathe fire.

Dragons look rather like dinosaurs. But dragons are only **MAKE-BELIEVE**.

This is a Chinese fighting dragon.

Some dragons are very old and wise. Others can fly.

Some dragons love treasure. Make up a play about a dragon.

29

MAKE IT YOURSELF

Please ask an adult to help you with these projects.

GROWING BEAN SEEDS

1 Put some soil in a pot.

2 Make holes in the soil about 2 cm apart, using a pencil.

3 Put one bean seed in each hole.

4 Cover the seeds with soil.

5 Water the seeds so the soil is damp.

6 Put the pot in a warm place.

7 Remember to water the seeds a little every day.

8 Watch your plants grow.

RECYCLING PROJECT

Collect aluminium drink cans.
The cans are aluminium if they do
not stick to a magnet. You can recycle
or sell aluminium cans. Find out
more at http://www.thinkcans.net

GLOSSARY

Aroma A nice smell.

Cereal A grain plant, such as wheat, maize or rice.

Extinct No longer existing, like the dinosaurs.

Fumes The used gas that comes out of a car.

Isle Another word for island.

Litter Rubbish.

Pollution Something that poisons the environment.

Recycle To reuse.

Sprig A shoot from a plant.

Unripe Not ready for picking or eating.

INDEX